MIDLOTHIAN PUBLIC LIBRARY

3 1614 00206 3254

P9-CCG-922

His Brown Horse

MIDLOTHIAN PUBLIC LIBRARY
14701 S. KENTON AVENUE
MIDLOTHIAN, IL 60445

BY TORA STEPHENCHEL

His brown horse
lives in the barn.

His brown horse
loves to play.

His brown horse
blinks in the sun.

His brown horse
runs in the field.

His brown horse
eats carrots.

His brown horse
swishes its tail.

His brown horse
drinks cool water.

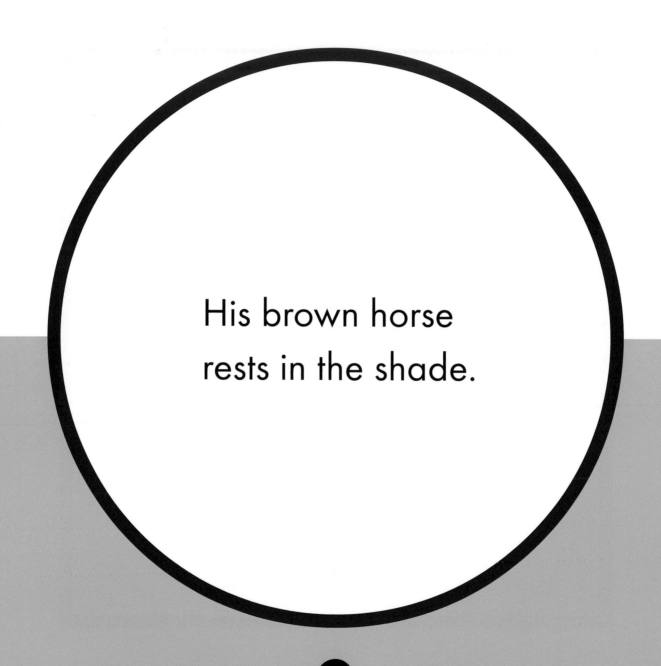

His brown horse
rests in the shade.

His brown horse
runs some more.

His brown horse
is loved.

Note to Caregivers and Educators

Sight words are a foundation for reading. It's important for young readers to have sight words memorized at a glance without breaking them down into individual letter sounds. Sight words are often phonetically irregular and can't be sounded out, so readers need to memorize them. Knowing sight words allows readers to focus on more difficult words in the text. The intent of this book is to repeat specific sight words as many times as possible throughout the story. Through repetition of the words, emerging readers will recognize, and ideally memorize, each sight word. Memorizing sight words can help improve readers' literacy skills.

brown

his

horse

About the Author

Tora Stephenchel lives in Minnesota. She loves to spend time with her son, daughter, husband, and two silly dogs.

EASY NON FIC 428 STE

The Child's World
childsworld.com

Published by The Child's World®
1980 Lookout Drive • Mankato, MN 56003-1705
800-599-READ • www.childsworld.com

Photographs © Alla-Berlezova/Shutterstock.com: 6; ANGHI/Shutterstock.com: 10; Audrius Merfeldas/Shutterstock.com: 23; Dado Photos/Shutterstock.com: 13; horsemen/Shutterstock.com: 5, 9, 18; R. Rose/Shutterstock.com: 14; Stokkete/Shutterstock.com: 2; Tra' Cee/Shutterstock.com: 17; Vasyl Syniuk/Shutterstock.com: cover, 1, 21

Copyright © 2021 by The Child's World®
All rights reserved. No part of this book may be reproduced or utilized in any form or by any means without written permission from the publisher.

ISBN 9781503845015 (Reinforced Library Binding)
ISBN 9781503846548 (Portable Document Format)
ISBN 9781503847736 (Online Multi-user eBook)
LCCN 2020931173

Printed in the United States of America